Praise for *Search* from Nonprofit Leaders

"The shortest distance between you and a good job in the nonprofit sector is reading this book. It takes you through each step—from realistic numbers about the scale of the nonprofit sector and how to begin your job search to negotiating a salary and ending the search. Like a fine gem, the value of this book far exceeds its size."
> **Barry Gaberman, Senior Vice President**
> **The Ford Foundation**

"Larry Slesinger has written a marvelously practical and informative book. Although its utility goes far beyond the nonprofit sector, the book is essential for the growing number of people who are finding the cause-oriented world of work more rewarding."
> **Raul Yzaguirre, President and CEO**
> **National Council of La Raza**

"*Search* is chock-full of suggestions. Experienced professionals looking for a nonprofit job will find the tips on managing a successful job search especially helpful."
> **Diana Aviv, President and CEO**
> **Independent Sector**

"Those of us in the nonprofit arena know that it's a very special place to be, with exceptional challenges and great satisfaction. Since finding the right job fit is key, the clear and practical information found in the pages of *Search* will be incredibly valuable to all readers."
> **Jan Verhage, Executive Director**
> **Girl Scout Council of the Nation's Capital**

"*Search* is a down-to-earth, straightforward road map for landing a senior position, including CEO, in a nonprofit organization. For those wishing to transition from government service or the for-profit sector, Larry Slesinger provides expert tips on how to leverage your experience and expertise."
> **John H. Graham IV, President and CEO**
> **American Society of Association Executives (ASAE)**

"At last! A practical guide for people seeking employment in the nonprofit world. . . . Larry Slesinger's counsel is wise and generous. . . . His candor as well as his thoughtfulness is refreshing. And the book is a pleasure to read."
William M. Dietel, former president
Rockefeller Brothers Fund

"Larry Slesinger offers concise, straightforward, and insightful advice on how to seek—and find—the right job in the nonprofit arena."
Peter D. Bell, President
CARE

"Increasing the flow of talent into nonprofit organizations is one of the most important steps to strengthening the sector. *Search* is an excellent and pragmatic guide for people seeking to effectively apply their skills and experience at a nonprofit."
Mario Morino, Chairman
Venture Philanthropy Partners

"Some books take hundreds of pages to tell you how to find a job. Slesinger's book is mercifully short—a small gem that will tell you quickly what you need to know."
Joyce Henderson, Ed.D., Vice President for Human Resources
Volunteers of America

"More and more people are seeking ways to make a difference in society and are turning to the nonprofit sector as a way to do it. But the transition from a for-profit business to a nonprofit organization can be difficult. In *Search*, Larry Slesinger has provided a roadmap for navigating the switch. He provides important, practical strategies that can lead to a rewarding nonprofit career."
William D. Novelli, CEO
AARP

"Larry Slesinger knows that of which he writes. A seasoned professional in the realm of nonprofit management and a consummate matchmaker in the executive search world, Larry provides counsel that is right on. Read, follow your dream—and enjoy making a difference while making a living."
Patricia Riley Johnson, Founder and CEO
Rebuilding Together/Christmas in April

Search

Winning Strategies to Get Your Next Job in the Nonprofit World

Larry Slesinger

Piemonte Press

Search: Winning Strategies to Get Your Next Job
in the Nonprofit World

by Larry Slesinger

Published by Piemonte Press
PO Box 639, Glen Echo, Maryland 20812
301-320-0680
www.MyNonprofitJobSearch.com

Cartoons by Mark Litzler (MLitzler@saint-lukes.org)

Publisher's Cataloging-in-Publication
(Provided by Quality Books, Inc.)

Slesinger, Larry.
    Search : winning strategies to get your next job in
the nonprofit world / Larry Slesinger. -- 1st ed.
    p. cm.
    LCCN 2003098061
    ISBN 0-9746657-5-4

    1. Job hunting. 2. Nonprofit organizations.
I. Title.

HF5382.7.S56 2004   650.14
                  QBI03-200837

Contents

About the Author

L arry Slesinger, the author of *Search*, is founder and CEO of Slesinger Management Services, a firm that provides executive search and other management services to nonprofit organizations. His work draws on his own experience as a senior manager of nonprofits, including playing a major role creating and building BoardSource (formerly called the National Center for Nonprofit Boards) in Washington, DC.

Since creating his firm in 1998, Mr. Slesinger has completed numerous searches for foundations, associations, and other nonprofit organizations, primarily in the Washington area. Most searches have been for chief executive officer, chief operating officer, chief financial and administrative officer, and other senior staff positions. An up-to-date list is available on his website at www.SlesingerManagement.com.

Prior to launching his firm, Mr. Slesinger served as special assistant to the president of the Inter-American Foundation, program officer of the John and Mary R. Markle Foundation, vice president of BoardSource (then called the

National Center for Nonprofit Boards), and vice president of the Carnegie Endowment for International Peace.

Mr. Slesinger is the author of *Self-Assessment for Nonprofit Governing Boards* and co-author of the first edition of *A Snapshot of America's Nonprofit Boards: Results of a National Survey*, both published by BoardSource. He has also written articles on the job-search process; they are posted on his website.

Mr. Slesinger is a member of the Career Services Advisory Council of the Greater Washington Society of Association Executives (GWSAE) and a former member of GWSAE's Compensation and Benefits Survey Advisory Council. He is also a former member of the selection committee of the Washington Post Award for Excellence in Nonprofit Management, administered by the Washington Council of Agencies, and a former governing board member of the International Development Conference and IONA Senior Services.

Mr. Slesinger has a bachelor's degree from Carleton College and an MBA from the Stanford University Graduate School of Business. He and his family live in Bethesda, Maryland. He can be contacted via his website, www. SlesingerManagement.com.

Foreword

A t last! A practical guide for people seeking employment in the nonprofit world. In 40-plus years of working in this arena, I have had countless inquiries from friends, friends of friends, relatives, and even strangers I've encountered on planes and at meetings about how they could get a job with a foundation or a nonprofit. How can one possibly give a responsible answer to such an inquiry in only a few minutes? You can't do it and be helpful. And yet the need is real and often pressing.

This book is the answer to the problem.

One of the most rewarding things about working in the nonprofit sector is the opportunity to assist people who believe that they, too, might find a deeply satisfying work experience in this sector but who haven't a clue as to how to begin the process of seeking employment in this foreign environment. Throughout my career I have been impressed with the readiness—indeed, the often eager readiness—with which my colleagues were prepared to respond to requests for career assistance. It is as if by joining this universe of people, you automatically take on a responsibility to extend and deepen the nonprofit sector's search for a more diverse workforce and increase the professional experience and competency of its staff members.

The women and men who run our foundations and nonprofits lead and manage a critical part of the national economy, and their contributions are essential to the improvement of the commonweal. The need for lively, engaged, dedicated, bright people to join our ranks will grow significantly in the decades ahead.

This concise book promises both to inform and to assist those who would like to become a part of the dynamic independent sector. Larry Slesinger's counsel is wise and generous, and he has a clear understanding of this unusual marketplace. His candor as well as his thoughtfulness are refreshing. And the book is a pleasure to read.

William M. Dietel
Former President of the Rockefeller Brothers Fund
President of the Pierson-Lovelace Foundation
Chairman of the F.B. Heron Foundation

What This Book Will Do for You

This book will help you get the job you want. It's written especially for people who want a leadership position in a nonprofit organization—those who would like to be executive director or who seek a senior staff position such as deputy director or director of a key department. But much of the advice will be useful as well for professionals looking for less-senior positions at nonprofits. And the book may even help those seeking jobs—senior or junior slots—in business or other sectors of the economy.

Many people are skilled at carrying out the job they currently have and quite capable of performing well in the job they'd like to get. But they don't know how to get that job. Or they don't know how to find openings that would interest them.

Every day I hear from people who are ready to look for a new job. They may be hoping to leave a job they've had for several years, or they might have left a job recently and not yet found a new one. They may be thinking of a major career shift—for example, leaving the world of business or retiring from government service or the military—and they want to work for a nonprofit organization. Their common question is: "How do I begin my search?"

This question is especially prevalent among people who have had successful, stable jobs with one employer for many years. They are competent people who have accomplished quite a bit in their careers. They're seasoned and sophisticated. But they don't have much experience looking for jobs. They don't have a resume that puts their best foot forward, they don't handle interviews well, or they don't know how to build a network that will provide valuable information. They may not even know they need a network—despite the fact that it's often the single most important factor in a successful job search.

This book is for them—and for you, if you want a leadership position at a nonprofit.

If you already have a leadership role and are looking for new leadership responsibility, you're probably busy and don't have time to read long books. I've made this book as concise as possible so you can begin—immediately—to do the right things to help you get the right job.

Let's get started.

CHAPTER 1

Defining the Nonprofit Sector

"The overriding mission is not to make money

but rather to solve a problem at the community,

national, or global level."

The term "nonprofit sector" covers an incredibly broad range of organizations with many types of jobs at the senior level. If you want to work for a nonprofit, you're probably motivated by a desire to support a cause with a social or public purpose. You might have a passion for the arts and want to work for a museum. You might be concerned with the state of housing in low-income neighborhoods and wish to be part of a community development organization. You might be concerned with the incidence of HIV/AIDS, or heart disease, or cancer, and would like to be at an organization that conducts research to cure diseases or assists people with serious illnesses. Or you might be committed to improving the conditions of people in poor countries and want to work for an international development organization. For all of these organizations, and the many others in the nonprofit sector, the overriding mission is not to make money but rather to solve a problem at the community, national, or global level.

As noted in *The New Nonprofit Almanac* by Independent Sector (the national coalition of many of America's most significant nonprofits), the nonprofit sector includes hospitals, museums, schools, homeless shelters, symphony orchestras, research centers, youth groups, advocacy groups, and many other kinds of organizations. Unlike government agencies, these organizations are private. Unlike businesses, they are exempt from certain taxes, most significantly income taxes. ("Nonprofit" is something of a misnomer, as these organizations are allowed to generate revenue that exceeds expenses —the definition of "profit." But they do not pay taxes on this surplus, and the organizations have no owners who can convert the surpluses into personal wealth the way successful business owners can. Peter Drucker has recommended calling these groups "social sector organizations," a more positive term than nonprofit, not-for-profit, or tax-exempt. But Drucker's phrase has not yet caught on, so I'll stick with the more generally accepted term "nonprofit" in this book.)

According to Independent Sector, the United States is home to 1.6 million nonprofit organizations that employ 11.7 million people—about nine percent of the U.S. labor force. Nonprofits' total revenue was recently calculated to be

$665 billion—more than the gross domestic product of South Korea, Russia, Indonesia, or Australia.

If you want to work for a nonprofit, you're probably thinking of one of the following three types, as classified by the Internal Revenue Service:

• **501(c)(3) organizations, which have a charitable, educational, or scientific mission.** There are some 734,000 of these in the United States, ranging from the American Red Cross to the Museum of Science and Industry in Chicago to the San Francisco Food Bank.

• **501(c)(4) organizations, which do a significant amount of advocacy work on behalf of certain issues and causes.** Their work often includes lobbying to influence legislation. There are some 140,000 of these groups, including the American Civil Liberties Union, the National Rifle Association, and the Sierra Club.

• **501(c)(6)s, which are trade associations and professional societies organized to represent and serve the interests of a particular trade, industry, or profession.** There are 80,000 of these, such as the American Institute of Architects, the California Medical Association, and the National Association of Home Builders.

Many of these nonprofits have little or no paid staff, so the number of potential employers is considerably below 1.6 million. But there are still enough jobs at these nonprofits to offer a range of worthwhile career opportunities.

Another segment of the nonprofit sector that attracts tremendous interest from jobseekers is the grantmaking foundation—organizations like the Ford Foundation, the Baltimore Community Foundation, and the Kellogg

LITZLER

"WHY DO WE CALL IT THE NON-PROFIT SECTOR ANYWAY? THAT MAKES US SOUND CARELESS OR LAZY."

Foundation—that disburse money to other nonprofits. These foundations often have endowments and use the investment income to finance their grantmaking; some foundations raise money that is then given to other nonprofits in the form of grants.

The grantmaking foundation community is truly small. According to the Foundation Center, there were 62,000 grantmaking foundations in the United States in 2001. Most are run by unpaid staff such as family members or trustees. In the Foundation Center's latest survey of 20,000 larger foundations, only 3,360 reported having paid staff. The total number of staff positions at these 3,360 organizations was 17,800—far fewer people than work for Microsoft (50,000) or Hewlett-Packard (150,000).

Of these 3,360 grantmaking foundations, most have small staffs.

Number of paid staff	Number of foundations
1-2	2,107
3-4	588
5-9	401
10-19	141
20 or more	123

As you can see, only 123 foundations in the entire country have staffs with 20 or more people, and only 264 foundations have staffs of 10 or more. Large, well-known foundations such as Ford, Rockefeller, Kellogg, MacArthur, and Packard, each of which has more than 100 employees, are truly the exceptions. In the Washington, DC, area, where I live, one of the most influential and best-known grantmakers is the Eugene and Agnes E. Meyer Foundation; it has a staff of only 16 people.

It's certainly worth including foundations in your search for a job in the nonprofit sector. But it would be a mistake to focus on them exclusively, given how few jobs they encompass—and how little turnover they typically experience.

The Vast Nonprofit Sector

Type	Number of Organizations
501(c)(3)	734,000
501(c)(4)	140,000
501(c)(6)	80,000
Religious congregations	354,000
Other nonprofit organizations	319,000
Total	1,627,000

(For detailed statistics and analysis, see *The New Nonprofit Almanac and Desk Reference* by Independent Sector (www. IndependentSector.org) and the Urban Institute, published by Jossey-Bass.)

Why It's Tough to Get a Job at a Grantmaking Foundation

	Number of Organizations	Number of Employees
Entire nonprofit sector	**1,627,000**	**11,664,000**
Wal-Mart	1	1,300,000
McDonald's	1	413,000
FedEx	1	185,000
Starbucks	1	62,000
Microsoft	1	50,500

continued on next page

Why It's Tough to Get a Job at a
Grantmaking Foundation (cont.)

	Number of Organizations	Number of Employees
Nike	1	22,700
Maytag	1	20,600
La-Z-Boy	1	17,850
Foundations reporting paid staff*	**3,360**	**17,800**

*There may be foundations that have paid staff and did not participate in the Foundation Center survey. But if all had responded, the total number of employees would still be less than many large corporations and less than one percent of total nonprofit employment. For more information, see *Foundation Staffing, 2003*, published by the Foundation Center and available at www.fdncenter.org/research/trends analysis.

CHAPTER 2

If You're New to the Nonprofit World

"Finding a leadership position is always a challenge,

especially for people who do not already have

nonprofit experience. But it is possible."

T he nonprofit sector is frequently attractive to people who no longer want to work for a for-profit business or in other areas of the economy. I often hear from people who have lost jobs at corporations as a result of layoffs or who have reasonably secure jobs but simply want to apply their skills to mission-driven organizations. Similarly, I hear from people who are ready to leave government after a long career or a short-term political appointment and from others who are about to retire from the military but not ready to stop working completely. In all of these cases, people are looking for work that is socially meaningful, even if it might include a reduction in income.

Finding a leadership position is always a challenge, especially for people who do not already have nonprofit experience on their resume. But it is possible, as several of my successfully completed searches confirm.

The following are the keys to breaking into the nonprofit sector at the senior level:

• **Focus on jobs in which the required skills are similar to those in positions you've held outside the nonprofit sector.** Many of the clients for whom I've conducted searches for chief operating officer or chief financial officer recognize that people who've held similar jobs in corporations or elsewhere are great prospects. They correctly conclude that running an accounting department in a company is not unlike doing it in a nonprofit, even if some of the accounting jargon and rules differ. Positions in fundraising, on the other hand, are often perceived to have characteristics that do not exist outside the nonprofit sector, which makes it much more difficult to enter the sector via this path. But there are always exceptions. Some nonprofits recognize, for example, that successful fundraising draws on skills that anyone who has done well in sales or marketing has already mastered.

• **Be explicit about the most important skills you have acquired that can readily transfer to the nonprofit sector.** This could mean talking about your sales and marketing track record when you pursue a fundraising job or about staff supervision experience for any senior-management role that involves overseeing others.

• **Look for nonprofit organizations with a history of hir-**

LITZLER

"SO YOU'VE TRIED THE PUBLIC
SECTOR AND THE PRIVATE SECTOR.
YOU'RE RUNNING OUT OF SECTORS."

ing senior people from outside the sector. Obviously, these organizations—and the people there who have business, government, or military experience—are more likely to recognize the relevance of your skills than are organizations where the senior staff has worked primarily at nonprofits. The network you develop to find appropriate openings can help you identify these organizations and these people.

• **In your resume, cover letter, and conversations with potential employers, highlight any board or other volunteer experience you've had with nonprofits.** Demonstrate that your interest in the sector is not, say, a temporary one that might pass as soon as the economy improves.

• **Don't generalize based on your experience with the first nonprofits you contact.** I've led some searches for chief operating officer (COO) and other senior management positions where the clients strongly prefer candidates with business experience. And I've had other clients with similar openings who have preferred candidates with nonprofit experience, ideally in an organization with a similar mission. In both cases, I've seen organizations ultimately select a person who did not fit their initial preference. Searches are dynamic, unpredictable, and, most important, not over until an offer has been accepted.

Breaking into the Nonprofit Sector

• Focus on functional jobs that you've already mastered, such as controller or editor.
• Identify your skills that transfer easily to a nonprofit.
• Look for nonprofits with a tradition of hiring "outsiders."
• Highlight volunteer experience with nonprofits.

CHAPTER 3

Organizing Your Search

"Your search needs a structure."

To succeed in your search, you need to think of it as a campaign: a set of activities you carry out to accomplish a single goal. In this case, your goal is to get one good job in the nonprofit sector. The numerous activities to reach your goal—identifying openings, building a strong network, writing a compelling resume, enlisting effective references, etc.—are the subject of most of the rest of this book.

Your search needs a structure. Especially if you have a full-time job or children to raise—or both—it's all too easy for

LITZLER

"YOU KNOW TURNOVER IS HIGH
WHEN THEY STOCK RESUME PAPER."

days and even weeks to rush by without your doing much to advance your search. But even if you are not employed and have relatively ample time to work on a search, you still need to organize yourself to put your time to best use.

Create, in effect, a campaign headquarters—the place where you can sit and think about your search, make calls and send emails to advance it, and keep in one place all the information you'll be gathering. The best place for your headquarters is at home, where you presumably have at least a desk, computer, and telephone. The key elements of your headquarters are the following:

• **Telephone.** Consider investing in a separate phone line with voicemail. You don't cast a professional image if somebody trying to reach you has to speak with a young child who may or may not pass along an important message...or if the caller hears a voicemail greeting geared more toward family and friends...or when a potential employer gets a busy signal because somebody at home is on the Internet. A personal wireless phone would avoid all these problems.

• **Email account.** Similarly, you need an email account with a professional address. It's OK to share the address with other family members since no potential employer or other key contact would know that. But you don't want an unprofessional or otherwise distracting address such as SpringsteenFan@aol.com or EddieandMarie@yahoo.com. A more prosaic email address, like the kind you have at work, is much more appropriate.

If you can access your office email at home, you can consider using that as long as doing so doesn't violate email usage rules at work. Just make sure your exchanges won't be seen by anyone else at the office, such as a personal assistant who might have authorized access to your account.

• **Calling cards.** You can use your business card from work. But if you're currently unemployed, or you want calls to go primarily to your home office (or your mobile phone), or you want emails to come to your personal or family account, then you should purchase a small batch of cards with all your contact information. Since your phone number(s) and email address are the key items, be sure they're easy to read. Also list your home address and, obviously, omit your current job title and employer's name.

• **Tracking system.** If you are successful at creating an effective network, you will soon have a substantial number of people to contact and job openings to investigate. You need a system to keep track of this steadily growing and changing information. The high-tech solution is a computer database such as Access or contact-management software such as Act! A simple low-tech solution is a three-ring binder; each page can track your communications with a particular person in your network or with a potential employer. No matter what method you choose, keep a record of each person's name and contact information, key items you and that person have discussed, and next steps. This system doesn't have to be fancy; it just has to organize essential information.

• **Office hours.** Unlike work projects and many family activities, your job search is conducted mostly in private. Nobody will know if you go three days without sending a resume. Nobody will care that you haven't followed up on a lead suggested by a member of your network. Nobody will nag you if you haven't responded to an ad in the *Chronicle of Philanthropy*. That's why a search requires tremendous focus and self-discipline. To help you concentrate on all the essential but usually mundane tasks, set specific hours when you will conduct your search. The commitment might be two hours every Sunday, or an hour every night, or as much as three hours each morning. Regardless, this is time in which you will not allow yourself to be distracted by office work, television, Internet surfing, or other competing activities. Establish a schedule and then stick to it.

• **Budget.** Although conducting a search does not cost a lot of money, it's not free. You may need to subscribe to an essential newsletter that lists job openings in your area of interest, purchase a new phone line dedicated to your search, print business cards, take a few people to lunch or coffee, purchase a new blouse or shirt and tie, and perhaps travel to another city to see some key people.

With the possible exception of this last item—travel— none of these expenses should be back-breaking. But they can add up to at least a few hundred dollars, and you might find yourself wishing you didn't have to incur them, especially if you're not employed and are short of cash. Keep this in mind: Given the total salary you will receive over the course of a few years in a good job, this investment in your search is small compared to the staggeringly high returns it can produce.

Essentials for Campaign Headquarters

• Telephone with professional-sounding voicemail
• Email account
• Calling cards
• Tracking system
• Office hours
• Budget

CHAPTER 4

Focusing Your Search

"To search effectively, you must know

what you're looking for."

When people ask me for help with their job search, my typical first question is, "What do you want to do next?" Sometimes they reply only that they're interested in a good opportunity or want to work for an organization that makes a difference. I am completely unable to respond to such vague and wide-ranging objectives.

To search effectively, you must know what you're looking for. Being focused will help you determine the best ways to spend your time and, just as important, will help people in your network give you useful advice and information.

Being focused doesn't mean that you have a specific employer in mind or that you will never deviate from your plans as the search unfolds. But it does mean you have some criteria to guide your search.

Four key search criteria

1. Location. Do you want to remain in the geographic area where you live? Is there a specific city to which you'd like to move? Or are you truly flexible and willing to consider various locations?

2. Mission area. Do you want to work in the arts, or housing, or health, or education, or international development, or...? The more specific you are, the better you'll be at learning about organizations that will appeal to you most.

3. Functional area. Do you want to work in fundraising, program or service delivery, marketing, day-to-day operations, finance, human resources, or any other specific functional area that is a typical part of a nonprofit? Are you interested exclusively in chief executive positions, or will you consider any other position at an organization? Again, by being more specific, you'll get faster at finding the right opportunities to explore.

4. Compensation requirements. How much money do you want to make in your next job? How much money do you need to make in your next job? Although the answers to these two questions should not be the same, you must think about both—especially the second one.

I recommend identifying a target salary range that reflects your past earning history and what organizations are currently paying for the kind of job you want. Salary informa-

LITZLER

"I LIKE THE FASTER THAN A SPEEDING BULLET AND POWERFUL AS A LOCOMOTIVE SKILLS BUT HE STILL SEEMS LIKE A SQUARE PEG WE'RE FORCING INTO A ROUND HOLE."

tion in the nonprofit sector is readily available through a number of public sources, listed in Chapter 11. Once you have the range in mind (of course, the minimum figure is most important, since you're not going to turn down a job that pays above your range), use that as a guide to determine which jobs and organizations to pursue. Keep in mind that the range is only a guide. Naturally you hope you won't have to accept a job below your target minimum, but you might decide to do so if there are compensating factors, such as very generous employee benefits or an extraordinary opportunity to work with a premier organization.

Be focused—but also be flexible

As you develop your key search criteria, keep in mind that you can have multiple and even contradictory objectives. For example, you might want to be the CEO of a small nonprofit or a very senior staff member of a large nonprofit. Or you might be interested in jobs in fundraising, membership, and communications. Or you might want to explore opportunities in Washington, DC, Boston, and San Francisco. The key is to bring some specificity to your requirements and aspirations. Being open to anything simply means you will find nothing.

Establishing these criteria will give you needed focus, but don't be so rigid that you fail to be open to attractive opportunities that fall outside your parameters. Obviously, if you see something unexpected that you want, you should pursue it. Nonetheless, your ability to define what you want— and to communicate that to others—will help you find real opportunities.

Focusing Your Search

Specify your requirements or preferences regarding:
- Location
- Mission area
- Functional area
- Compensation (salary and benefits)

Then be flexible enough to consider opportunities that fall outside these specifications.

CHAPTER 5

Finding Openings

"People who think good jobs

never get advertised are simply wrong."

T o find openings in the nonprofit sector, you need to draw on a wide range of resources. The two most productive are your personal network and advertisements. Many jobseekers also try to learn about openings from executive search consultants, also known as recruiters or headhunters.

Your network

The network you create and maintain during your search is by far your most important tool. In fact, it's so important that I've devoted the entire next chapter to the topic.

Advertisements

People who think good jobs never get advertised are simply wrong. As a search consultant, I advertise all my openings. It's also wrong to think that nobody ever gets a good job by responding to an ad (perhaps because you think the job has already been filled) or that only someone with connections will get serious consideration. When I'm conducting a search, I often interview people who lack a recommendation from somebody I know. Sometimes I'm so impressed that I then recommend them to my client, and sometimes they get the job.

You should systematically read all the periodicals and websites that are most likely to publicize job openings of interest to you. There is no master list in the nonprofit sector—not even of openings in one metropolitan area. So you need to stitch together a number of sources. Increasingly these sources appear online. Some charge, but many are free. A few even allow you to register for an alert service; this automatic service sends job announcements that meet your criteria as soon as the ads are posted.

The following sources specialize in openings in the non-profit world:

- www.ExecSearches.com
- www.CEOupdate.com (mostly trade associations and professional societies)
- www.idealist.org (especially for jobseekers early in their career)
- www.PhilanthropyCareers.com
- www.asaenet.org (see Career Headquarters)
- www.associationjobs.org

- www.cof.org (see Career Center for jobs at grantmaking foundations)
- www.fdncenter.org/pnd/ (see Job Corner)
- www.developpro.com
- www.nonprofitcareer.com
- www.nonprofitjobs.org
- www.pnnonline.org (see Career Center)
- www.ISOjobs.com (for health care)
- www.DotOrgJobs.com
- www.npxpress.com
- www.nassembly.org (health and human services organizations)
- www.NonprofitOyster.com
- www.DeepSweep.com
- www.NPTimes.com (see employment marketplace)
- www.OpportunityNocs.org
- www.interaction.org (jobs in international relief and development)
- www.InternationalJobs.org
- www.dev-zone.org (international)
- www.ReliefWeb.net (international)
- www.devnetjobs.org
- www.WashingtonJobs.com (search under Industry for Associations, Foundations, and Nonprofit for job openings plus search advice)
- www.wcanonprofits.org (jobs in Washington, DC)
- www.mdnonprofit.org (jobs in Maryland)
- www.pnp-inc.com (jobs in the New York City metro area)

Do not overlook daily newspapers (and their online editions) such as the *Washington Post* and www.Washington

Post.com. The paper typically includes several ads for associations and other nonprofits under Professional Opportunities in the Sunday business section.

For an up-to-date list of the best websites that focus on jobs in the nonprofit sector, go to my website at www.SlesingerManagement.com. If you come across a website or

"IRONIC THAT THE JOB OPENINGS ARE ONLY A PAGE AWAY FROM THE COMICS."

other resources I should add to my list, please notify me by email at Larry@SlesingerManagement.com.

Executive search consultants

Knowing that I'm a headhunter who specializes in non-profit organizations, many people call me when they're looking for a new job. They're especially interested in knowing "what's out there." My response usually disappoints them. I explain that I'm so focused on the searches I'm doing at the moment that I'm typically not aware of many other openings.

Search consultants don't represent jobseekers—we get paid by the employer, not the person looking for the job. Whether our specialty is nonprofit or for-profit searches, the way we work is the same: We focus on our current clients' requirements.

That said, consider this anecdote. When I was in my own job search several years ago, I tried hard to meet a particular search consultant who had great credentials in the nonprofit sector and, even better, was a friend of a close colleague who knew of my plans. Despite that connection, the consultant ignored my letter and follow-up phone calls; I never got past her assistant. Then, around 10 one Monday night, my home phone rang—and it was the headhunter. "Larry," she said, "I have your resume, and I know (mutual friend) has suggested we meet. I'm about to launch a search and think it might interest you. Would you be free for lunch this week?"

So if you know of search consultants with expertise in the nonprofit sector, feel free to send them your resume—especially if you have a mutual acquaintance who can make introductions. But don't badger them for a meeting. Don't be upset if you're completely ignored. And don't be shocked if they call out of the blue weeks or months later.

My advice, in sum:

• Do look at all relevant websites and periodicals regularly to know what's being advertised.

• Don't spend too much time trying to get the attention of search consultants. If you can manage this easily, terrific, but recruiters are not your most efficient or dependable source of leads.

• Do invest the majority of your time and energy into learning about openings from your network. The flow of information won't be as fast as looking at a website, but the quality will be much higher because it will come from people who know you, know employers, or both. Your network, I predict, is how you will get your next job. Learn more about how to build and use this valuable group of people in the next chapter.

The Smartest Ways to Allocate Your Search Time

Source	Portion of Your Time
Building and using your network	80%
Ads on websites and in periodicals	15%
Executive search consultants	5%
Total	100%

CHAPTER 6

Establishing and Cultivating Your Network

"You don't have to be a wildly extroverted, life-of-the-party

type to build a great network of informants....

You simply need a systematic approach."

W hen I was in a job search early in my career, I learned from a member of my network about an opening that had not been advertised. When I called the organization to inquire, the first question was "How did you know about this?" Identifying my contact boosted my credibility—and soon I was offered an interview and subsequently the job. By the way, I had never actually met the person who told me about the opening. He was simply a friend of a former boss who was willing to pass along a valuable piece of information to someone he knew only via a resume and a brief phone conversation.

Your ability to get a job depends on several variables: your track record in the positions you've held so far, your skill at identifying openings, the strength of your resume and cover letter, your interviewing skills, the quality of your references, and your salary aspirations.

But none of these comes close to the importance of your network. Your network is made up of people who know you are ready for a new opportunity and can possibly contribute to that effort. These people include current and former colleagues, friends, and—very important—colleagues of colleagues and friends of friends (and colleagues of friends and friends of colleagues—people whom you do not yet know but will soon meet and add to your network).

Why a network is so valuable

Your network—or, more precisely, the people you put into your network—can do several things for you.

• **Identify openings that might interest you.** No one person—not even the most highly regarded search consultant in town—knows of all job openings. But everyone knows of at least one opening. It might be at this person's own organization or at one where a friend, colleague, spouse, or partner works. It might be because this person noticed an ad about the opening. It might be because the organization with the opening has asked this person to help identify candidates. Regardless of the reason, everyone knows about some opening somewhere.

• **Put in a good word on your behalf.** Because so many employers depend on recommendations from trusted sources, you significantly increase your chances of being invited for an initial interview when a member of your network can recommend you. Then, once you've had an interview or two, this person may be able to serve as a reference. This assumes, however, that the person knows your work well and can speak authoritatively. I don't take this for granted since many people in your network will be recent acquaintances who are not appropriate references, even though they can do other useful things.

• **Provide intelligence about potential opportunities.** They can give you insights into a particular organization, position, or person—insights that will help you tailor your pitch and even help you decide whether some openings are worth pursuing. Many jobs sound great on paper, especially at places with attractive public images. But a member of your network can discreetly tell you about lesser-known internal characteristics that are important to know.

• **Keep your spirits up.** Looking for a job is rarely easy; you should expect scores, or even hundreds, of disappointments before the search ends successfully. There will be some moments—especially if you're without a job—when you just need to be in touch with another person who's not going to turn you away. By simply talking to you and trying to be useful, people in your network can help you remain positive and keep moving ahead.

You don't have to be a wildly extroverted, life-of-the-party type to build a great network of informants. And you don't need a bulging Rolodex at the outset of your search. You simply need a systematic, disciplined approach to identifying people who might be helpful and a willingness to take the initiative to remind them periodically that you're still looking.

Creating and working an effective network

1. Write out a list of 40 people. These should be the individuals who are best equipped to tell you about openings, provide general intelligence, put in a good word at the right moment, or help keep your spirits up. Obviously, you should exclude people who, if they knew you were searching, could leave you vulnerable at work. In any case, consider people who:

- work where you currently work,
- worked with you in previous jobs,
- used to work where you work now,
- know you through professional associations or alumni groups,
- know you through community activities,
- got to know you in college or graduate school, or
- live in your neighborhood.

Coming up with 40 names might seem daunting at first, but don't be discouraged if it takes more than a few minutes to put together a list. This exercise is most useful when it stretches your thinking beyond the obvious group of colleagues and friends.

The key: Think broadly, but place the most emphasis on the 40 people who are both most willing to help you and best positioned to be useful.

2. Write to the 40 people on your list. I suggest sending each one a personalized letter (by mail or email). Do this

LITZLER

"IN MY NETWORK OF PEERS
AND COLLEAGUES YOU'RE A
PRIME TIME SITCOM."

over a four-week period. Write to the first 10 during the first week, the second 10 the next week, and so on. Enclose your resume along with a brief cover letter explaining what you'd like to do next and your hope that they can help identify potential openings or other people you should contact. Close the letter by saying you'll follow up in a few days with a phone call.

Make it clear that you are not asking them for a job. Since

most will not have an opening that matches your skills and experience, you don't want them to misinterpret your request, say they have nothing, and shut the door.

3. Call to schedule a short talk—in person, if possible. Ask if you can meet for a brief (20- to 30-minute) conversation. If a face-to-face meeting is not possible, talking by phone is an acceptable, albeit less than ideal, alternative.

If you can meet the individual in person, suggest doing it over coffee, not over lunch or another meal. You should be busy talking, listening, and taking notes, none of which is easy to do while eating. In addition, finding time for coffee (which can take place at any time of day) is much easier than scheduling lunch, and you'll also take less of your contact's valuable time.

4. Ask about openings or further contacts. For your meeting, take another copy of your resume in case your contact doesn't bring the original along. Open the conversation by describing your objectives: what your ideal next job would be like or perhaps your primary one or two areas of interest. Then ask your contact if he or she knows of any openings that might meet those objectives.

If the person does have an opening or two to tell you about, get all the particulars and find out whether you can or should mention the person by name if you decide to pursue the openings. But don't be surprised or disappointed if the person has little or nothing to offer. Even when contacts don't know of a potential opening now, they may hear about something a few days later and will likely remember to tell you.

Whether your contacts suggest openings or not, also ask them the key question that will help you build your network:

"Can you identify at least three other people whom I should contact to discuss my search?" Like the initial 40 members of your network, these do not have to be people with jobs to offer. They just need to be useful members of your network. Find out the relationship your contact has with each person and whether you should use the contact's name when you write the new person to ask for a meeting.

5. Repeat the contact cycle with the new names. Send your letter and resume via mail or email, follow up by phone, meet over coffee, pursue leads of possible openings and new names to contact. If after a month you've talked to all 40 people on your initial list and each has given you three names, you will have 120 new names. That's a total of 160 people in your network, many of whom you did not know at the outset. Even if you reach only half of your initial 40 and each of these 20 people gives you only two names, you'll have 40 new names to add to the initial 40. Keep this up for a few months and the numbers will continue to expand. You may even have trouble following up in a timely way with all the new names that continue to emerge and the suggestions that each person offers.

That's when you know your network is working.

Of course, you shouldn't pester the members of your network or waste their limited and valuable time. That's why you get your letter and resume to them before calling and why you want to meet briefly over coffee instead of lunch. But don't let the relationship stop there. As helpful as your contacts want to be, they don't wake up each morning asking themselves, "What can I do today to help that person I talked to last week find the right job?" Many will forget, so it's important to remind them periodically that you're still looking.

After you complete the initial round with contacts, send them an email every 60 days or so to quickly let them know that you haven't yet found the right job and to see if they have new ideas. I found one of the best jobs of my career when I informed one of my contacts, for the third time over the course of several months, that I was still looking. He had several helpful suggestions the first two times, but none had materialized into the right fit, and neither had anyone else's. But this third time he told me, "Glad you called. Yesterday we announced the creation of a new organization and the appointment of its first executive director. She'll be looking for a deputy; let me pass your material to her." I got that deputy job a few weeks later.

If you have qualms about contacting people, here's a simple plan to help you overcome this reluctance. Establish a routine in which you commit to doing the following every day, Monday through Friday:

1. Call at least five people per day.
2. Email at least five people per day.
3. Meet face-to-face at least two people per day.
4. Remind them. Check in every two months.

I can assure you that almost everyone in your network will want to help. Some will be of marginal benefit or even useless. A few will actually be very helpful. One will be of incalculable value. So establish, build, and cultivate your network with confidence.

After you find the job you want

Even when you end your search, your network will still have value. It will include some people who might be helpful colleagues in your new job and many who will be useful in your next search—which you hope won't be soon, but one never knows. So don't abandon this new set of contacts once you're done looking. At a minimum, send them all a note when you complete your search, tell them how it ended, and thank them for their help.

The network I'm advising you to create is designed to build a group of people who know you're in the market and will tell you about opportunities you might not hear about otherwise. The steps listed above to create, expand, and maintain the network focus on continually adding new people—people who are valuable for many reasons, not because they are likely to offer you a job.

In creating and expanding your network of contacts, your goal is to let everyone know—to the maximum extent possible—that you're available. The only limitation should relate to your current employment situation. You obviously don't want to inform somebody about your search if the news will get back to your office, and especially your supervisor. Given how few degrees of separation exist between people, you do need to ask your contacts to be discreet. The conventional wisdom is that it's better to look for a job when you have a job, but there are clear advantages to looking when you don't have one. One is the freedom to be explicit with everyone about your goals.

You've heard the saying "It's not what you know—it's who you know." But in finding the right job, "It's not who you know—it's who knows you." Networking is the best way to quickly expand the number of people who know you and know you're available.

Final note

Just as this book was about to be published, the website www.LinkedIn.com was getting good publicity as a useful way to build a network for various purposes, including job-hunting. I plan to test it soon for the searches I'll be leading, and suggest you consider using it for your own job search.

The Value of a Network

1. Identifies other people to add to your network.
2. Identifies job openings.
3. Recommends you to potential employers.
4. Gives you insights into the job market, specific organizations, and openings.
5. Keeps your spirits up.

Creating Your Network

1. Identify 40 people.
2. Write to them; then talk to them.
3. Ask them to identify openings you should investigate.
4. Ask them to recommend three people to add to your network.

Repeat Steps 2 to 4 until the search is over.

Maintaining Momentum

Each week:

1. Call five people per day.
2. Email five people per day.
3. Meet with two people per day.
4. Remind everyone in your network every 60 days that you're still looking.

CHAPTER 7

Creating a Great Resume

"Remember: At this stage,

the purpose is not to get the job

but to get the interview."

Your resume is a critically important document. Although a good one won't assure you of getting the nonprofit job you want, a bad one will guarantee that you won't get serious consideration.

The purpose of a resume is simple: to convince the reader very, very quickly that you have enough relevant skills and experience to merit an interview. So remember: At this stage, the purpose is not to get the job but to get the interview.

A resume's most important characteristics

For a typical search, I receive 100 to 300 resumes, and I read them all. Here's what I like to see.

• **Clarity.** Your resume needs to help me understand what you have done. I want to know where you studied, where you've worked, when you were there, and what your skills are. A career counselor or book on resume writing can help you explore the many possible ways to structure a resume clearly. For example, if you fear it will be hard for prospective employers to translate the career you've had in the world of for-profits, the military, or government into a nonprofit setting, you may want to use a functional resume that emphasizes what you do rather than where you've done it.

That said, I have a strong preference for a chronological resume, with the most recent job first, because it shows me at a glance the path you've followed. Since I'm especially interested in knowing where you've worked and how long you stayed with each employer (or with each job within one organization), I don't like functional resumes' long lists of skills. In fact, I wonder if the functional resume is being used to divert my attention from something I think is relevant, such as where you have actually worked and how long you've been at each job.

• **Results.** I'm especially interested in knowing what you've accomplished, especially in your most recent jobs. I'm also looking for results that are impressive and memorable. The more you can quantify, the better. Here are two examples of how to improve the way you write about results:

Mundane: "Produced the annual report."

Much better: "Redesigned the production process for the

annual report so that it reached our members earlier than ever before in our organization's history—and at a 20 percent reduction in cost."

Mundane: "Oversaw the annual audit."

Much better: "Implemented new accounting system that led to the first annual audit without any adjustments in the history of the organization."

Too many resumes are dull. Stressing results is an effective way to make the document more interesting to read and to make you a person I want to meet.

• **Brevity.** Naturally you have much to be proud of and want me to know a lot about your career, education, awards, memberships, hobbies, etc. However, you must pick the most salient items so that the resume runs no more than two or three pages at most. Remember, I receive a lot of resumes and would rather not read anything longer than it needs to be.

On the other hand, I do not think you should limit your resume to one page, as some people recommend. There's just not enough space unless you use a small font that will strain my eyes and annoy me...or you make the margins so small that the document looks crowded...or you're just out of college and don't have many discrete items to list. It's much better to add a page than to create a resume that's a nuisance to read.

• **Honesty.** If you become a serious candidate, the employer will take steps to verify some of the information in your resume, so be sure everything is 100 percent correct. One obfuscation I do not like is the implication that you're still working when in fact you have left your most recent employer. If on the day you submit the resume you are no longer employed, then your date of employment should not say, for example, "1998 to present." Replace "present" with the final year—even if it's this year and you state in the cover letter that you recently left your job.

• **Flawless.** Make sure your resume contains no incorrect grammar, no word misspelled, no incorrect dates ("1992 to 1988" when you mean "1992 to 1998"), no inconsistent formatting. After you've proofed the document twice and feel certain it's perfect, ask a friend to read it and identify any mistakes, even the most trivial. Such errors are surprisingly powerful detractors from what would otherwise be a solid document.

• **Easy to read.** I want to absorb your information effortlessly. Again, take care to avoid anything that gets in the way of presenting information quickly: small fonts, tiny margins, an illogical way of listing items or sections, page breaks at the wrong places, etc.

A chronological resume's most important components

In your two- or three-page resume, I recommend listing the following items, in this order:

1. Contact information

• Name.

• Home address.

• Home telephone number. (Remember to use a professional greeting—no Elvis impersonation—and an adult voice on your answering machine.)

• Direct-dial office phone. Alternative: Use your wireless phone number if there's a risk that a potential employer could leave an indiscreet message with a receptionist or assistant.

• Email address. This is especially helpful to potential employers who prefer to conduct some communications electronically. Obviously, you should select an email address that is secure. If you aren't comfortable listing your office account, then use a personal account—ideally one you can access from your office since you don't want to wait all day to see important messages.

2. Employment

If you're writing a chronological resume, start with your most recent employer. Include:

• Name of employer.

• City and state.

• Your title.

• Dates showing when your job began and ended. Usually it's sufficient to tell the years only, so write "1995 to 2000," not "August 1995 to November 2000."

• A concise description of accomplishments. See the sample resume at the end of this chapter for an example of how to list these.

3. Education

Starting with your most advanced degree, include:

• Name of institution and its location.

• Degree and major.

• Year you obtained degree.

• A concise list of academic honors or special achievements, such as "summa cum laude" or "president of campus chapter of Habitat for Humanity."

4. Honors and Awards

List anything truly impressive that's not already included under Employment or Education. Being selected as Volunteer of the Year by the local Red Cross chapter is a great honor that deserves mention. Being included in *Who's Who in the East* is not.

5. Publications

List articles, chapters, and books that you wrote (and that you can easily provide to potential employers if they ask). If you are the co-author of anything you list, make that clear.

6. Memberships

List professional associations that are relevant to your career; especially note key responsibilities, such as chairing a committee. But keep this list brief. Belonging to an association in your field shows your interest in professional and career development, which is worthy. Still, it's not as if you've been elected to an exclusive club.

7. Additional Information

If you have something vital to add that doesn't fit above, put it here. However, I recommend against listing hobbies, providing your height and weight, telling your exercise regimen, verifying that your health is good, stating your marital status, identifying your spouse or children, or adding other items that do little or nothing to enhance the resume. So what qualifies as an exception? Something that distinguishes you and might be interesting for the employer to ask about in an interview—for example, that you ran in the last five New York City marathons or serve as first violinist in a community orchestra. But don't worry if you don't have anything to list here. Saying nothing is better than including an item that is commonplace.

8. Date

End your resume with the month and year—such as

"January 2004"—so readers will know how current the document is. This is especially helpful for hiring organizations when resumes get filed and then circulated months or even years later, at which point the reader does not realize the document may be incomplete. Change your resume's date every four months or even more frequently so it doesn't look stale or raise questions about why you haven't found a job yet.

What about references?

I suggest omitting these completely from your resume. After an interview you'll have a better idea of which references the employer should call and when they'll be contacted. And don't bother to say that references are available upon request. Employers just assume that. For more on references, see Chapter 10.

What about a job objective?

I've seen many resumes that begin with one- or two-sentence objectives. Often they're vague and even meaningless ("a challenging opportunity that will draw on my leadership skills"). I recommend omitting an objective and instead using the cover letter to state why a particular job meets your goals.

Fine points of mailing and emailing

When you're mailing your resume:

• Print it on standard copy paper (20-pound white), not thicker paper or paper that is gray, cream, or some other color. All these things get in the way of making photocopies, which employers need to do if they want others to see your resume.

• Send it flat, not folded for a #10 business envelope. Again, this saves time, especially if employers need to feed it into a photocopying machine. It also looks better without the folds.

These days, however, most resumes come to me via email as an attachment. I actively encourage this, but not every employer wants attachments. When you're not sure, ask. If you're emailing:

• Use hard page breaks and sufficient top and bottom margins so that if and when the resume is printed, no text will shift to a new page.

• Most important, use software that is common. Today, Microsoft Word is far and away the best because it's so widely used. A PDF file is also good since you're assured that the recipient can't change the formatting and text. In any case, be sure your recipient can open your file.

To learn more about resume writing, any good library or bookstore will offer several books that go into great detail, including showing various formats. To get a quick, low-cost, candid assessment of a resume you've already drafted, consult the resume review services at www.ExecSearches.com or www.NonprofitProfessionals.com.

No matter what approach you take, remember this:

When I read a resume, I ask myself one fundamental question: Do I want to invest the time to talk to this person? Concluding that I do usually takes two minutes at most. Deciding that I don't takes just 30 seconds.

Your goal: Make sure that I want to keep reading after 30 seconds, that I think highly of you within two minutes, and that your resume moves right to the top of my "people to interview" stack.

An Effective Chronological Resume

This is an example of a well-written, well-designed chronological resume. Use it as a starting point for creating a document that captures you, not as a rigid template showing the best or only way. (Although the organizations' names are real, the rest is fictitious; nobody by this name—or any other—did all these things.)

Notes about the resume:

❶ Direct line is best.

❷ Use wireless (rather than home) number if you can't trust your kids to take messages.

❸ Clear and businesslike.

❹ Implies Robin still works there.

❺ Budget and staff size indicate this isn't a tiny outfit.

❻ Good use of numbers (since a 50-percent increase in donors could mean going from four to six).

❼ Clearly a successful fundraiser, but also a good boss/mentor.

❽ Promotions indicate mastery of various jobs.

❶ Robin H. Smith
2154 Woodmont Street, Pittsburgh, PA 15217
Office: 412-123-1234 (direct) / Wireless: 412-123-2154
Email: RobinSmith@earthlink.net **❷**

Experience   **❸**

___

1999 to   **American Red Cross, Southwestern Pennsylvania Chapter**
Present   **Pittsburgh, PA**
         Vice President for Development
❹   Direct all fundraising for 10th largest Red Cross chapter in the
         United States; staff of 50 and budget of $4.5 million. **❺**

         Accomplishments
         • Increased donations from individuals, foundations, and corporations
         by 75 percent over four years (from $1.8 million to $3.15 million).
         • Expanded number of individual donors by 45 percent (from 1,555
         to 2,257), primarily by conceiving and launching Have a Heart **❻**
         campaign to attract new donors under the age of 35.
         • Persuaded William Royal Foundation to make its first-ever grant
         over $100,000 to support disaster assistance training program.
         • Increased development staff from 2.5 to 4; created training program
         that has been replicated by other Red Cross chapters to strengthen
         fundraising capacity of mid-level development staff. **❼**

1992 to   **Cleveland Museum of Art**
1999   **Cleveland, OH**
         Director of Membership and Development (1996 to 1999)
❽   *Director of Membership* (1993 to 1996)
         Membership Coordinator (1992 to 1993)
         Increasing responsibility for membership and fundraising for major
         cultural organization.

         Accomplishments
         • Restructured individual membership program that increased
         renewal rate from 63 percent to 77 percent, and increased dues
         revenue by 40 percent.
         • Created corporate membership program, in which 60 percent of
         Cleveland's largest companies participate, providing 25 percent of
         the museum's unrestricted revenue.
         • Developed and carried out fundraising strategy that led to the
         museum's first grants from major foundations outside of Ohio, i.e.

Continued on next page

⑨ Board experience is always useful for CEO and other senior positions.

⑩ Clearly a low-level job; no need to give it much space.

⑪ Indicates good work performance.

⑫ It's OK to skip Honors and Awards if nothing is worth mentioning.

⑬ Publication in the *New York Times* would be more prestigious, but this article's topic will generate interviews and stimulate conversation.

⑭ A judgment call: Exotic travel is unlikely to be relevant, but it gives Robin an unusual dimension.

⑮ Working with kids shows another positive dimension.

⑯ Don't let this get more than four months out of date.

LITZLER

"THE LAST ITEM ON YOUR QUARTERLY WORK PLAN SHOULDN'T BE 'UPDATE RESUME.'"

six-figure support from Ford Foundation, Pew Charitable Trusts, and Kellogg Foundation.
• Staffed and energized board development committee, which historically had been underutilized but now plays key role in corporate membership program. ⑨

1991 to   Ketchum
1992   New York, NY
⑩ *Client Services Assistant*
At major public relations firm (8th largest world-wide), assisted account executives working with organizations including the Metropolitan Opera, American Express, and the New York Transit Authority. Attended firm's highly regarded two-week "PR boot camp" for staff new to the profession. Earned 15 percent   ⑪ performance bonus at end of first year of employment. Represented firm at job fairs at colleges on the East Coast.

Education

New York University, B.A., Communications, 1991
Assistant director, WNYU (campus radio station) and on-air host of
    weekly program about New York City arts and culture.
Junior year in Barcelona, Spain.

Memberships

⑫ American Association of Museums (founding member, New
        Audiences Task Force, 1997-1999)
Squirrel Hill Arts Coalition (Board of Directors, 2000-Present)

Publications

"Why I Love to Raise Money—Even When They Say No."
NYU Alumni Magazine, April 2002.   ⑬

Additional Information

⑭ Extensive travel throughout Australia, New Zealand, and the islands
        of the South Pacific.
Fluent in Spanish.
Volunteer coach of children's soccer team.
                                                    ⑮
(February 2004) —⑯

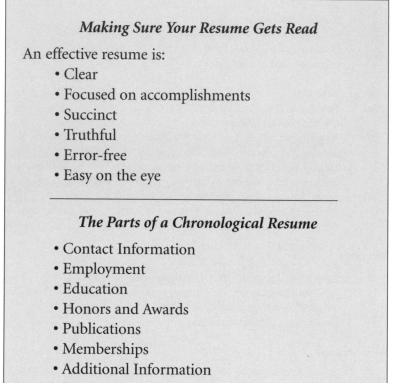

Making Sure Your Resume Gets Read

An effective resume is:
- Clear
- Focused on accomplishments
- Succinct
- Truthful
- Error-free
- Easy on the eye

The Parts of a Chronological Resume
- Contact Information
- Employment
- Education
- Honors and Awards
- Publications
- Memberships
- Additional Information
- Date

CHAPTER 8

Writing Persuasive Cover Letters

"Most cover letters are weak and do nothing

to help advance the writer's candidacy."

Hundreds of people send me resumes without cover letters—even when the job announcement specifically requests one. I guess they figure I know what they want (the job I'm filling) and assume their resumes let me know they're capable of doing the job. What they don't realize is that without a cover letter, I don't know why they want a particular job or what makes them especially qualified for it.

The cover letter is as important as your resume in your search for a great job with a nonprofit. Nevertheless, it is a very different document to write well and deserves special attention. In the end, it will take more of your time during the job-search process than your resume.

As discussed in the previous chapter, the resume is meant to describe you, especially what you've accomplished at work and what educational credentials you've earned. It's a brief document that, once written, has some permanence to it. You don't necessarily have to change it daily, and you can send more or less the same document to a diverse set of potential employers. Usually it's written independently of any specific opening.

The cover letter is the appropriate and essential place to link yourself to the organization you are trying to impress. Like the resume, the letter's purpose is not to get you the job but to get you an interview. You can't know whether the reader will go over the cover letter before or after the resume (even if the letter's on top, sometimes we look at the resume first). But you can be sure you won't be considered for an interview until both documents have been read carefully.

A cover letter's most important characteristics

Most resumes I receive do come with cover letters. But most cover letters are weak and do nothing to help advance the writer's candidacy. Here are the characteristics of the best cover letters.

Tailored. Strong cover letters address the specific opening. They explain exactly why you're interested in it, why you're qualified to do it, and what you will do to follow up. A customized letter demonstrates that you know something about the organization (maybe from research you just did on its

"MY WORRY IS THAT YOUR COVER LETTER IS SO GOOD DUE TO ALL THE PRACTICE YOU'VE HAD."

website) and about the position (maybe that it's the logical next step in your career, given the responsibilities you've held recently).

Almost as bad as excluding a cover letter is sending one that is clearly a form letter. When it's obvious that you inserted the name of the organization and position into a letter that basically talks only about you, then I can reasonably conclude that you are also applying for five or 50 or 500 other jobs—that what I am offering is not necessarily of great interest to you except that you found it in a list of many other openings. This doesn't hurt my feelings. But it does tell me you don't care enough to take the time to show me why you and this particular opening are a good fit.

Literate. The cover letter is an excellent opportunity to demonstrate your writing ability. It's especially good for showing that you can write persuasively, which is always a good skill regardless of the position. In contrast, a resume is not as good for displaying your way with words. Not only is the typical resume heavy on phrases and lists, but it's always possible that your resume was actually written by someone such as a career counselor (which is OK to do).

Concise. One page is usually fine; two pages are acceptable; anything longer is unnecessary. The following three-part structure works well:

1. Begin the letter by identifying the opening by title and organization. (Especially when recruiters are involved, they might be filling several positions simultaneously; don't make us guess which one you're interested in.)

2. Explain why the job interests you and, more important,

why you offer what the employer wants. In other words, state explicitly the "what I can do for you" angle.

3. Conclude by stating how you'll follow up, perhaps by calling in a week to confirm receipt.

Connected. There's no question that personal connections help. They don't guarantee that you'll get the job or even the interview. But they help distinguish you from the many other candidates. So if you know that I know Mary Johnson, begin your letter by saying, "Mary Johnson suggested I contact you because she thought my skills and experience would be a good match for the chief operating officer position you're filling at Organization X." This significantly increases your chances that I will seriously consider interviewing you. But if you don't have a connection, don't fret. You'll still get considered if you have a strong cover letter and resume.

The best cover letter is the one that makes me say to myself, "I want to meet this person—pronto."

An Effective Cover Letter—and an Ineffective One

On the next page is a strong cover letter from fictitious Robin Smith, whose resume is in the previous chapter. Following it is a cover letter that fails on many counts—and was actually sent to me from an applicant interested in one of my searches.

Notes about the cover letter:

❶ Smart to start out by naming a mutual professional friend.

❷ Ties employer needs to Robin's experience by emphasizing local fundraising.

❸ Shows awareness of relevant local news.

❹ Demonstrates other key attributes of an executive director (even though Robin has never been a CEO).

Robin H. Smith
2154 Woodmont Street
Pittsburgh, PA 15217
412-123-1234 (office)
412-123-2154 (wireless)
RobinSmith@earthlink.net

February 15, 2004

Mr. Joseph Brown
Chairman of the Executive Director Search Committee
Pittsburgh Chapter of the American Cancer Society
909 Penn Avenue
Pittsburgh, PA 15219

Dear Mr. Brown:

❶

I was glad to learn from Sally Barnes that the Pittsburgh chapter of the American Cancer Society is looking for a new executive director. Given my track record in raising money from a wide variety of individuals, foundations, and corporations in western Pennsylvania, I am confident I can be an effective CEO for the American Cancer Society and am pleased to submit this application.

❷

From reading your job announcement, I realize that you're looking for a leader who can build your donor base. That's precisely what I've done over the past five years at the Southwestern Pennsylvania chapter of the Red Cross, where I am vice president for development. I know how to get current donors to increase their gifts, and I know how to persuade new donors to support important causes. Given the publicity surrounding the new University of Pittsburgh study on the effect of carcinogens on the water quality of Pittsburgh's rivers, even more people in the region should be ready to consider supporting the American Cancer Society. **❸**

I also have the broader management and leadership skills you are seeking in a CEO. I have extensive experience working closely with board members (a current Red Cross board member formerly served on your board and can serve as one of my references at the appropriate time), and I know how to build a strong staff.

❹

Continued on next page

❺ A tug at the heartstrings: Personal experience adds to Robin's motivation.

❻ Paragraph accomplishes several tricky things: acknowledges request for salary requirements, does not answer the question, but supplies impressive alternative information.

❼ Always good to speak of next steps, including taking initiative to follow up.

❽ Overall impression: The writer is interested in the job, offers impressive relevant experience, and is too smart to send a form letter.

I also have a strong personal interest in the mission of the American Cancer Society. My father passed away from stomach cancer five years ago. I know that he and my mother greatly appreciated the information and support they obtained from the South Florida chapter when he became ill. **⑤**

Your job announcement asked for salary requirements. I'm confident that you will be offering a salary that's competitive with CEO positions at comparable organizations. My preference is to discuss my expectations after learning more about the position. But I can tell you that the Red Cross has recognized my value to the organization by increasing my salary significantly. When I joined the Red Cross in 1999, I started at a salary of $55,000. Five years later, I'm now earning $82,000, which represents an increase of more than 10 percent per year. **⑥**

I hope that I will be able to meet with you and your colleagues on the search committee to discuss how I can help strengthen the Pittsburgh chapter of the American Cancer Society. I will contact you in one week to confirm that you received this letter and to see if I can provide you with any additional information. **⑦**

Thank you. **⑧**

Sincerely,

Robin H. Smith

Enclosure

Notes about the cover letter:

❶ Unforgivable to misspell the contact's name.

❷ Fails to identify the job being applied for, which may cause confusion.

❸ Doesn't identify where accomplishments took place; hiding something?

❹ Rife with cliches and jargon.

❺ Overall impression: Obviously a form letter, and a weak one at that. The writer can't communicate clearly and didn't care enough to tailor a letter to this job's requirements.

Making Sure Your Cover Letter Gets Read

An effective cover letter is:
- Tailored
- Literate
- Concise
- Explicit about referrals and personal connections

January 22, 2004

Mr. Larry Slesinger
SLESINGER MANAGEMENT

Dear Mr. Slensinger: ❶ ❷

Entities today must maximize their financial positions with a strong balance sheet and cash flow position in order to qualify for capital financing and growth. Consider these accomplishments: ❸

• Revenue Cycle/Cash Management aggressive re-engineering $2M extra cash.
• Increased cash flow over 100% and raised credit ratings.
• Drove net operating margin from negative to an attractive positive result while maintaining/gaining market share with excellent customer service.
• Captured $750K lost cash through strategic attention to detail and operational efficiencies/opportunities. ❹

Please contact me whereby allowing for an in-depth discussion how my integrity, accuracy, technical/analytical savvy, and high work ethic can take your entity to the next level of performance.

Sincerely, ❺

Terry -----

CHAPTER 9

Acing the Interview

"A bad interview dooms all chances of demonstrating

the many leadership and management skills you possess."

If you're invited to an interview with a nonprofit organization, you'll probably have 30 to 90 minutes to persuade the employer that you're a strong candidate. Although there's no correlation between interviewing well and success on the job, you do need to perform impressively at this meeting. And "perform" is definitely the right word. An interview is not simply a meeting or a conversation. You are on display as the interviewer judges whether you possess the skills and experience to do the job well and a personality that's appealing. Ultimately, the employer will give the thumbs-up to only one person.

Accept this fact, but recognize that the interview is a chance for you to learn about the employer as well. You might find that the people, or the surroundings, or the exact nature of the work once it's described in more detail offer less than what you want in your next job. It's far better to learn this now, bow out, and move on than to accept a position you want to leave a few months later.

I've spent many hours with search committees interviewing candidates for CEO positions. These committees are typically seeing the top eight or so people out of an applicant pool of 100 to 300 people. It's disheartening that so many of these candidates—who clearly are successful at their jobs—fail at this key stage. Typically, only two of the eight finalists excite the committee and remain under serious consideration. For the rest, a bad interview dooms all chances of demonstrating the many leadership and management skills the applicants possess.

Whether you're interviewing before a search committee or just one person representing the potential employer, there are five important steps you can take to increase the chances you'll perform well and pass this important test.

1. Tie your past to their future. The employer will ask you a number of questions about your skills and experience, which will tempt you to give chapter and verse about all the great things you've done. Before you submit to temptation, remember this: Interviewers don't care what you did elsewhere—they probably don't even know much about those organizations. What they care about is what you can do for them.

So do tell about your success in developing a new source

of revenue, or influencing a key piece of legislation, or implementing a new strategic plan. But then move on quickly—very quickly—to why this accomplishment will help you be a successful staff member for them.

2. Be concise. Many interviews, especially those with members of a search committee, begin with an icebreaker question such as "Please take three or four minutes to tell us about yourself." This doesn't mean they want to know where you were born. When you hog the floor—giving a detailed account of every job you've held since college—you keep them from more important questions they won't have time to ask.

So when you get this common question, try a brief, targeted reply like this: "You have my resume, so I won't walk you through it. But as I think about my career, I realize how much I love to build/lead/manage/turn around organizations. Becoming your next CEO/vice president/director of development is a logical extension of the path I've followed over the past few years. That's why I'm here today, and I hope I'll have time to elaborate over the coming hour."

If they then want a 15-minute soliloquy, they'll ask for more details. But keep your answers brief. And keep their questions coming.

3. Know the organization. You're not ready to sit down for an interview until you've read key organizational documents that should be easy to get, such as the annual report, the IRS Form 990, the most recent audited financial statements, the strategic plan (assuming it's available to candidates; at a certain point in the process, it should be), the list of board members (if you're interviewing for the CEO or other very

LITZLER

"I SURE APPRECIATE ALL YOUR TIME INTERVIEWING, MEETING THE STAFF AND OUTLINING YOUR VISION. TELL ME YOUR NAME AGAIN."

senior position), and everything on the website. Don't be caught asking about anything you should have found out from doing your homework.

Assuming you know what you're talking about, don't be reluctant to demonstrate your command of a few key facts. You don't have to come off as an expert on all germane topics, especially since some interviewers won't know a lot of details anyway. But do make it clear that you understand the environment you may be entering.

4. Bring three questions. If you're concise, the interviewers will complete their agenda and let you use the remaining time to pose questions of your own. Don't pull out a folder containing a list—you're having a conversation, not taking a deposition. But do plan to ask three or so questions. These may be ones that emerged from what you've already been asked, what you've memorized, or what you've written on a small note card. Ask questions that show you have a strategic, creative, and curious mind. Good possibilities include "What are the most significant competitive pressures the organization will face over the next three years?" or "What does the leadership think is the most appropriate financial strategy for the next two years?" Then use the answers to drive home more reasons why you'd be a good CEO/vice president/department director for them. Concisely, of course.

5. Be animated. Think about the session from the interviewers' standpoint. If you're talking to the members of a search committee, they may be seeing eight people over one or two days. They're sitting the whole time. Getting up for yet another Diet Coke and a few pretzels becomes the highlight of the day, especially if some of the candidates perform poorly. Or if the interview is with members of the staff, they might be seeing other candidates that day or feeling anxious about getting back to a project that is due soon.

The interview is the ideal time for you to be a breath of fresh air. Be energetic without being in overdrive. Bring a warm smile, humor, and a sense of confidence and self-assurance. Shake hands with each and every person who's interviewing you, and don't appear to ignore anyone in the group when you're answering questions. If you're in the running for a CEO position, the interviewers are trying to decide if they want you to lead and represent the organization—that is, them—over the next few years. And if you're interviewing for a senior staff position, they're thinking about whether they want you as a colleague whom they'll work with every day for many years.

Even seemingly small things can undermine a successful interview. In the no-detail's-too-insignificant-to-overlook department, here is additional advice to help you perform well.

• **Come 15 minutes early.** I once arrived on time for a job interview only because I ran the last three blocks. My perspiration and breathlessness made this all too obvious.

• **Stop by a restroom or someplace with a mirror before you enter the meeting room.** Check your necktie, lipstick, hair, etc. I remember when the members of one search committee commented on the red lipstick on a candidate's teeth—they found it distracting and questioned whether she could represent the group in public.

• **Accept a glass of water if offered a drink.** Even if you don't expect to get thirsty, it's handy to have when you need a few seconds to think before speaking.

• **Turn off your cell phone.** Or if you must keep it on, explain why at the outset. (You could say, for example, "As you know, I currently work at the White House and must be reachable at all times by the chief of staff.")

And finally, don't even consider uttering the phrase "think outside the box." It's OK to be the only candidate who doesn't mouth this ever-present cliche. It might even get you the job!

Doing Well in the Interview

At the strategic level:

1. Connect your past to the interviewer's future.
2. Be concise when answering questions.
3. Know the organization before you sit down.
4. Bring three questions.
5. Be animated.

. . .and at the tactical level:

1. Arrive 15 minutes early.
2. Stop by a mirror to check your appearance.
3. Accept a glass of water even if you're not thirsty.
4. Turn off your cell phone.
5. Avoid cliches.

CHAPTER 10

Recruiting the Right References

"Although employers will decide for themselves

if and when to contact references, you must be sure

your references are ready to be helpful."

When you arrive at the stage where nonprofit organizations are giving you serious consideration, they will want to speak with references to learn more about you and your work. Although employers will decide for themselves if and when to contact references, you must be sure your references are ready to be helpful. Here's what I recommend.

1. At the beginning of your search—while updating your resume and creating your network—identify four to eight people who would serve as your best references. They must

"THIS IS THE NICEST MOST FLATTERING LETTER OF REFERENCE! THANKS MOM."

be able to speak from first-hand experience about your work and willing to take the time to talk by phone with a potential employer. Keeping in mind that the most credible references are people who have worked in the same office as you, consider asking:

• Current or recent supervisors.

• Current or recent peers and subordinates, both of whom can provide useful perspectives—especially if your relationship with your boss isn't sterling. (Of course, your employment situation will dictate whether you're in a vulnerable situation if you ask colleagues in your current office.)

• Current or former board members and consultants who have seen your work first-hand.

• People from recent previous jobs or ones who formerly worked where you work now. If you do ask prior colleagues, remember that the more recent your experience with these people, the better. References that provide a rich picture of you from five or 10 years ago but nothing about your recent work will raise a red flag.

Much less valuable are so-called personal references—friends, neighbors, and relatives. (One candidate listed his ex-wife!) Not only are they probably unable to speak authoritatively about your skills, but they come with a built-in bias that makes them unlikely to be objective about your strengths and weaknesses.

2. Ask each person for permission to use him or her as a reference. Then ask what phone numbers or email addresses the employer should use. Let your references know you're at the beginning of your search and it could be weeks or months before they're contacted. (By the way, all of these people should be on your initial network list, so you'd be contacting them early on anyway.)

3. Create a one- or two-page document that identifies your references. For each person, include name, current title and organizational affiliation, and relevant phone numbers and email addresses. If you're listing a home phone number, be clear about that since it influences when the person can be reached. There is no need to include a mailing address. Finally, include a sentence or two explaining why this person knows you, such as "Was long-time executive director of Maryland affiliate of Habitat for Humanity; retired in 1999. Hired me in 1995 to be director of finance."

4. Do not send the list when you send your initial cover letters and resumes. Wait until a particular employer requests references. Then and only then, review the list to see if any name is inappropriate given the organization or position you are pursuing—if, for example, you know the employer doesn't have high regard for one of your references.

More important, think at this point about new names that will work well for this particular opportunity. Remember that the best references know not only you but also the employer. They can speak more substantively about the all-important fit between you and the position, and they have more credibility because the employer knows them. Perhaps you learn during your interviews that the employer once worked with someone you used to work with—someone who could be a good reference but just didn't happen to be among the top candidates on your initial list. If so, seek that person's consent to be included and then give the updated list to the employer.

5. After you submit the list, alert the references by email or phone that they might be contacted and thank them in advance for their prompt cooperation. This not only reminds them that their rapid response is important, but it also gives you a chance to find out if they're available in the coming days. For example, one reference might tell you that since she is about to go on vacation in Hawaii, the best time to be contacted is within the next 48 hours. You can then pass this information along to the employer.

6. Do not insist that references let you know if and when they've been contacted. Although some will take the initiative to notify you, this could be an imposition for people with busy schedules. You want to preserve their time for talking to employers, not for giving you updates.

7. Always be sure to close the loop. If you know your references have been contacted, be sure to tell them how the search ended—whether or not you were offered and then took the job. You also want to thank them warmly for their help. A sure way to sour references on you is to fail to show appreciation. No one likes to be taken for granted.

Managing Your References

1. Identify potential references when you begin your search.
2. Get their consent.
3. Get current phone numbers and email addresses.
4. Create a master list; for each name, include contact information and a brief sentence explaining your relationship.
5. Tailor your list to each opportunity.
6. Alert references when they're likely to be contacted.
7. Inform and thank all references when your search ends.

CHAPTER 11

Negotiating Salary and Benefits

"Exactly how you should respond to salary queries

depends on a number of factors."

Although salaries in the nonprofit sector are not as high as in the for-profit world, that doesn't mean that wages are necessarily meager. But neither are they uniform. Salaries range widely, based primarily on the size of the organization and local market conditions. In the Washington, DC, area, where I focus my search work, senior staff positions can often pay anywhere from $75,000 to $150,000. However, exceptions exist on both ends of that range. In general:

• Grantmaking foundations pay more than other nonprofits.

• Trade associations and professional societies pay more than nonprofits operating in the charitable or educational realm.

• National organizations pay more than groups working at the community level.

Finding out what jobs pay

As you research suitable openings, you can obtain salary information from several sources. At least three organizations conduct salary surveys for the nonprofit sector at the national level:

• Abbott, Langer & Associates (www.Abbott-Langer.com).

• American Society of Association Executives (www.ASAE net.org). See its Bookstore.

• GuideStar (www.GuideStar.org).

The most relevant salary surveys focus on specific metropolitan areas. In addition to checking Abbott Langer, ASAE, and GuideStar for their sub-reports on particular cities, look for sources relevant to your area. For example, Cordom Associates (www.CordomAssociates.com) and the Greater Washington Society of Association Executives (www. GWSAE.org) have salary data for the Washington, DC, metropolitan region. Several state associations of nonprofit organizations (including Florida, Louisiana, Maine, Massachusetts, Minnesota, and New York) conduct salary surveys; the website for the National Council of Nonprofit Associations (www.NCNA.org) has links to its members and their publications on compensation.

To get salary data for a specific organization, see its Form 990, which most nonprofits are required to file with the U.S.

Internal Revenue Service. The 990 is a public document that identifies the five most highly compensated persons at the organization. The fastest way to get this document is to go to www.GuideStar.org, a nonprofit organization that has put 990s online for you to see for free. Remember that the most recent figures could be one or even two years old, so current salaries are probably a bit higher than what you'll find there.

Addressing salary queries

Potential employers will want to know about your salary history and requirements. Neither of you wants to go too far down the hiring path if the job can't pay something close to the salary you want. But it's tricky to figure out just the right moment to discuss money—always a sensitive subject.

If the employer's ad requests your salary history or requirements, either answer when you submit your resume or acknowledge the issue by saying you prefer to address the subject later. But do not ignore the question. That makes it look as if you don't know how to follow instructions. Exactly how you should respond to salary queries depends on a number of factors.

When the job announcement provides the salary range

• If the published range is satisfactory, say so in your cover letter.

• If your recent salary has been a bit below the range, say so and provide your current figure, as this will show that the new job is a natural progression in your career.

• If your salary has been a lot less than the range, avoid providing a figure in your cover letter. It's likely to signal that you're not ready for the job or not worth what the new job is willing to pay. But when there are understandable circumstances, explain them. Perhaps you've been working in another part of the country where the cost of living is far less or in a field where salaries are typically below much of the nonprofit sector.

• If your salary has been higher—especially much higher —you may want to say explicitly what you've earned but quickly add that you can consider the top of the published range given how appealing the opportunity is. Or say that although you have earned more, salary is not your primary criterion and you can consider the published range.

When you don't know the salary range

This puts you in more complex terrain. If you provide your salary history or requirements, you risk making employers think that you're either too expensive for them or available for less than they're actually willing to pay.

When answering such an ad:

• If your research indicates your salary is in the right ballpark, provide your figures and say you're willing to negotiate.

• If you have no idea what the salary might be and don't want to risk listing a figure that could disqualify you, again, don't ignore the question. Instead say, "I would be happy to discuss a mutually satisfactory salary after we have the opportunity to talk about job responsibilities during an interview."

When working with a recruiter or an employer with whom you have personal connections:

• If you don't know what the job pays, ask. My job

LITZLER

" IT COMES WITH THE USUAL PERKS FOR A NON-PROFIT EXECUTIVE POS- ITION. SATISFACTION. APPRECIATION. HONOR. "

announcements typically do not include a salary range, but if a potential applicant inquires, I will provide it. Once you know the range, then my advice above applies.

• If you ask and the employer prefers not to provide a range—which I don't think is typical—I recommend providing your recent salary history. Then quickly add that your financial aspirations for the new job depend on a number of factors you hope to learn about and discuss in an interview.

At the interview

If you've been asked to interview and the subject of money has never come up, prepare yourself—it will soon enough.

When the interviewer asks for your recent salary history, I recommend answering forthrightly and then asking immediately what salary range the employer has in mind for the position.

• If the figures provided are significantly less than you hoped to hear, ask whether there is any flexibility in the range. You can add, "As interested as I am in your organization, I wouldn't be comfortable taking a salary cut," or "As I think about the next stage in my career, I'm hoping to increase my current salary at least 15 (or 20 or 25) percent."

• If it's obvious that the salary will not reach your minimum requirements, say so clearly—if not at the interview, then in a follow-up note a day or two after the conversation. At worst, the employer will appreciate that you are not wasting everyone's time. At best, the higher-ups may decide they need to increase the salary range so they can continue to consider you.

When the potential employer does not ask about your salary or initiate a conversation about what the job pays:

• You may ask about the job's compensation near the end of the initial interview. If you ask simply, "What does the job pay?" you'll get a response. But you might get a more satisfactory response by asking something like, "What do you expect to pay to attract and keep the best possible person for this position?"

• You may sense that it would be better to wait until a second conversation. That's fine. It might even be more strategic to wait. After several interviews, you may be of such great interest that the employer will consider paying you more than the initial target figure.

No matter who initiates the conversation about salary, do be prepared for this subject to arise at any moment. Know what you want to say both about your past and about your hopes for the future.

It's not sufficient to connect the salary you want to what you've made recently. For example, if you're thinking of moving from a law firm to a mid-level position at a non-profit, you might have to consider a reduction in salary— something you might be willing to accept in return for greater job satisfaction. If your most recent salary was at a job you left two months ago, the potential employer will realize that you no longer earn that amount and won't consider that figure as relevant as you might like. (By the way, I think the often-used term "salary requirements" is inappropriate and misleading; you never want to draw a line in the sand and look inflexible, and, anyway, you're not making the rules.)

Also, never justify your salary goals in terms of personal financial commitments. Don't say you need a certain amount of money to pay your mortgage or your children's private school tuition. No employer will hire you just so you can meet those obligations.

So what should you say when discussing what you hope to earn at your next job? I recommend tying the figure you name to your assessment of that job's responsibilities and requirements. Say something like, "As you've explained it, this job requires a good deal of specialized expertise. I can provide that, along with the drive to take the position to the next level. So my hope is for a salary commensurate with the value I have to offer, along the lines of $X."

No matter how the topic comes up, keep in mind that when potential employers tell you the salary range they're considering, you are under no obligation to indicate then and there whether that figure is acceptable. Again, if the range is well below what you're looking for, you may want to offer the responses I suggested above. But if you need time to weigh a figure, simply thank the interviewer for the useful information and move on to another subject for discussion. You could, for example, ask how often salary reviews are conducted. (If the answer is "Irregularly," request that your letter of employment state clearly when your initial salary will be reviewed.)

The role of benefits

Of course, salary is only part of compensation. Benefits have monetary value, too, and can vary widely from nonprofit to nonprofit. Key benefits that can improve the total compensation when the salary is less than ideal include:

• the employer's contribution to a retirement program;

• health insurance (including how much of the premium the employer pays);

• the number of days available for vacation and other time off; and

• career development opportunities, such as memberships in key associations or paid attendance to key conferences and meetings.

Remember: Virtually everything in a compensation package is negotiable. If you're not comfortable negotiating, it pays to read some of the many books that have been written on how to bargain so that both sides feel they've benefited from the final deal.

Putting salary in perspective

Finally, of course you have to weigh any salary offer against your financial needs. Never accept a job whose pay is so far below your requirements that you wind up feeling resentful or strapped. Even so, remember that compensation includes psychic income—the satisfaction you derive from the job regardless of its salary and tangible benefits. If you're attracted to the nonprofit sector, then you are undoubtedly motivated by the mission of certain organizations, and money is not the overriding factor in your career plans. Be sure you take time to consider psychic income when you assess the complete compensation package.

Smart Salary Strategies

1. Analyze relevant salary surveys.
2. Be prepared to speak intelligently about past and future pay.
3. Assess the value of benefits, including psychic income.
4. Don't be afraid to negotiate—but be realistic.

CHAPTER 12

If You Don't Get the Job

"Although the criteria for making it to the short list

are often heavily influenced by skills and experience,

the final decision is heavily influenced

by personal chemistry."

One of the great pleasures of conducting searches for nonprofit organizations is meeting so many interesting and talented candidates. And one of the great disappointments is telling most of them that the job has been offered to somebody else.

In my searches, the two to five candidates who got quite far in the process have usually been through a great deal—an interview with me, an initial interview with my client, perhaps a second interview with others at the client's organization, maybe lunch with the potential boss, plus calls from

LITZLER

" IF THEY BEGIN, 'DEAR NOT EVEN ON
THE SHORT LIST APPLICANT,' I PROBABLY
DIDN'T WANT TO WORK THERE ANYWAY."

colleagues to confirm they put in a good word as references.

Understandably, the candidates who were not chosen want to know why they didn't get the job, what they could have done that would have led to a better outcome, and what they should do differently when they pursue other jobs later. Basically, they're ready to beat themselves up, and I go to great lengths to disabuse them of the notion that they're failures. The facts are these:

• If you were among the final two or three candidates, you did much, much better than the overwhelming majority. In a pool that might contain as many as 100 to 300 applicants (and sometimes more), the 90 percent or so who don't even get an initial interview are the ones who need to examine their strategy.

• Although the criteria for making it to the short list are often heavily influenced by skills and experience, the final decision is heavily influenced by personal chemistry. Sometimes the client simply likes the other person more and would rather have that person on his or her team than you.

• The organization is striving hard to create a certain demographic profile among its staff, and in particular among its senior staff. Although they are clearly open to people who come from all genders, races, ethnic groups, age brackets, etc., and they will only select someone who is superbly talented, they can easily and understandably be attracted to a candidate who also helps them fill a gap in their staffing pattern.

• Money is a factor. They might have been quite attracted to you but more comfortable with another candidate who was available at 15 percent lower salary. Even if they knew you would be willing to reduce your financial goals, they might be nervous that you would soon look for a higher-paying job elsewhere.

• The process is deeply personal and subjective. It does not guarantee that the employer will get the best person—only the one the employer thinks will be the best person. Sometimes it turns out a few months later that the employer was wrong and wishes you had been selected. Maybe you'll be available then, or maybe you won't.

So if you (once again) made it to the short list and wonder why you didn't get the offer, realize that if you handled yourself well and acted professionally at all times, you are actually better off than before. Some of the people you have just met in the interview process can become part of your expanding network. Send notes thanking them for considering you and alerting them that you might be back in touch to get their advice. Then proceed in your search with persistence and patience.

Eventually you will get the job you want.

If at First You Don't Succeed

1. Don't beat yourself up if you made it to the short list but didn't get the job. At a minimum, you've expanded your network.
2. Do worry if you never get asked to come in for an interview.
3. Understand the subjectivity of the process and the influence of legitimate factors beyond your control.

CHAPTER 13

When the Search Ends

"Once there's nothing more to discuss, it's still healthy

to ask for 24 hours to sleep on the offer."

At some point, you will be offered a job with a non-profit organization. Ideally, it will meet most of your key criteria, and you will accept it with enthusiasm. But don't think you must accept the first offer that comes along. Unless you are in such financial straits that you can't go another day without a job, or your current job is so unbearable that anything else would be an improvement, please take at least 24 hours to consider the offer before accepting it. There is no need to say yes the moment you get an offer, even if you've been engaged in some negotiations about salary, job responsibilities, starting date, or other terms. Once there's nothing more to discuss, it's still healthy to ask for 24 hours to sleep on the offer. Most employers will respect your desire to think carefully about such an important decision—after all, they don't want you to act recklessly once you're on staff.

Use that day to reaffirm that the job is worth accepting. If you're still not fully satisfied with the salary, the rest of the compensation package, or some other aspect of the job, this is the time to negotiate these terms. You will never be in a stronger position to improve your circumstances than when you've gotten an offer and are weighing the entire package. Just don't be so greedy that the employers decide you're not the person they want on their team and withdraw the offer.

The position doesn't have to be perfect—in fact, if you think it is, you'll probably be disappointed a few weeks into it—but it does have to offer enough of what you want for the next chapter of your career. A good night's sleep, plus a conversation with a trusted friend, colleague, or family member, can help you think wisely about the opportunity.

That said, don't analyze the decision to death. All jobs have their imperfections, and this next one, even if it's better than what you're leaving, will have its flaws, too. Your research has probably identified the most likely problems. Once you've weighed the pros and cons, you may well conclude that the position's good features far outweigh its shortcomings.

And so you accept.

Your search is over.

But your campaign to find this great job is not yet finished.

LITZLER

"OF COURSE I'LL BE NEEDING THAT FIRST WEEK AS PERSONAL TIME TO THANK EVERYONE WHO HELPED ME GET THE JOB."

You now need to inform everyone in your network that you have found a new job and thank each one for helping. Tell all the people whom you asked for advice, whether they gave you any tips or not. They will be glad to know your search ended successfully and will appreciate your taking the time to share your good news with them.

You will also want to inform key people at organizations where you applied for jobs (even if they never called you back for a second conversation) so they know your search had a successful outcome and you're no longer looking.

Give all these people your new contact information so they'll know how to reach you at your new job. Some of the people in your network may well be useful once you start your new job. No matter what, this network will undoubtedly be the basis for the network you'll need when you're ready to launch your next search.

Even if that new search doesn't begin for three or five or seven years, the world is so small and so interconnected that many of these same people will prove to be critically important to the network you'll put together then.

When the Search Ends

1. Take at least 24 hours before accepting the offer.
2. Inform your network of your success and say thank you.
3. Inform everyone to whom you sent a job application, regardless of whether those potential employers turned you down, ignored you, or offered you a job you declined. Thank them, too.
4. Retain your database of everyone in your network so it's ready the next time you're looking for a new opportunity.

Resources to Support Your Search

This book has, I hope, given you a blueprint for launching and carrying out your search for a great job with a nonprofit organization. But if you want additional advice on the search process, numerous books and organizations can help you.

Books with career advice

There are scores of books to help you find a job. Some look at the whole process broadly; the classic example is *What Color Is Your Parachute?* Others focus on specific slices of the process, such as how to write a resume or anticipate interview questions. A good bookstore will stock many of these. Online, start with <u>www.Amazon.com</u>, <u>www.BN.com</u> (the Barnes & Noble site), or <u>www.Borders.com</u>.

Career counseling

Outplacement firms and other such organizations can be a good source of career advice. They understand the search process and will give you advice and candid feedback on your goals, resume, the way you present yourself, etc. Unless your employer is providing an outplacement firm at its own expense, however, you'll need to pay for this service yourself. If you engage a career counselor or employment agency, be sure to clarify what specific services will be provided and what they cost. Then get, and thoroughly check, references from former clients.

Resume critiques, writing, and editing

For a quick, relatively inexpensive source of advice on your resume or for more extensive resume rewriting, contact www.ExecSearches.com or www.NonprofitProfessionals. com to schedule a telephone consultation with an experienced nonprofit recruiter. At both websites, you also can find a number of free, concise, and useful articles on key topics on the search process.

Tell Me What You Think

The advice in this book is based on my own experience—experience with several thousand people who have contacted me about searches I've conducted for nonprofit organizations as well as those who've asked me for general job advice. The book is also based on my own experience job hunting in the nonprofit world.

I'm confident, however, that if you use this book to guide your own search, you'll come up with new ideas that are worth sharing. I welcome your comments. Please let me know if you think I need to revise anything or add something new. Your comments will help make future editions stronger.

In addition, I'd like to know if this book helps you find a good job. Please send me news of your success and let me know which pieces of advice were most useful.

You can contact me at <u>Larry@SlesingerManagement.com</u>. Thank you for reading. And good luck!

Tell Larry Slesinger
1. What was most useful in this book?
2. What job did it help you get?
3. How can the book be improved?

Do you want another copy of *Search* for yourself or for a friend?

Four ways to order—
1. **Online:** www.MyNonprofitJobSearch.com
2. **Mail:** Piemonte Press, PO Box 639, Glen Echo, MD 20812
3. **Telephone:** 301-320-0680   Pay with credit card.
4. **Fax:** 301-320-9471   Pay with credit card.

To buy 10 or more copies, inquire about quantity discounts.

Title	Quantity	Price	Subtotal
Search	_____	$16.95	$_____
	For Maryland residents, add 5% sales tax (85¢ per book)		$_____
		Shipping	$ 3.95 *(per order, not per book)*
		Total	$_____

Payment

❏ Check payable to Piemonte Press

❏ Credit card (Visa, MasterCard, American Express)

Card Number _____/_____/_____/_____

Name on Card _____ Exp. Date ____ /__

Your Name _____
(if different from above)

Address _____

City _____ State _____ Zip _____

Telephone (_____)_____-_____

Email Address _____